MW01701397

Improving business performance

ESI INTERNATIONAL
AN IIR COMPANY

PRECEDENCE DIAGRAMMING

SUCCESSFUL SCHEDULING IN A TEAM ENVIRONMENT

PROJECT MANAGEMENT NUTS AND BOLTS SERIES

Carl Pritchard

Published by

ESI International

4301 N. Fairfax Drive
Arlington, Virginia 22203

Printed in the United States of America
ISBN 1-890367-32-X

CONTENTS

Page

ABOUT THE AUTHOR

Carl Pritchard is the principal of Pritchard Management Associates and is a recognized project management speaker, author, instructor, and consultant. His recent projects include *Risk Management: Concepts and Guidance (2nd Edition)*, *The Portable PMP® Prep* (audio CD series with J. LeRoy Ward, PMP®), *Field Guide to Project Management*, edited by David Cleland, and the first book in the Nuts and Bolts series titled, *How to Build a Work Breakdown Structure: The Cornerstone of Project Management.* He was the principal architect of ESI International's acclaimed distance learning program in project management. He is the U.S. correspondent for the British project management magazine, *Project Manager Today.* He writes and presents on topics ranging from presentation techniques to strategic project management.

Mr. Pritchard is active in professional project management associations and is a certified project management professional (PMP®). He earned a B.A. in journalism from The Ohio State University.

Mr. Pritchard lives in Frederick, Maryland with his wife, Nancy, and two sons, Adam and James.

ABOUT THE REVIEWERS

Len Krapcha has more than 20 years of construction and teaching experience with the United States Navy. He developed, implemented, and instructed the navy's formal course on construction contract administration, quality control, and quality assurance. As the Engineering Aid Schools director, Mr. Krapcha supervised accredited post-secondary instruction to students in civil engineering technologies and quality control practices. He prepared job task inventories, individual skills assessments, and various occupational standards with the supporting curriculum for skills attainment.

As a senior engineering aide, he supervised staffs in quality control inspections, construction project planning and estimating, and construction materials design and testing. His last assignment with the navy was as a resource and program manager in a mobile construction battalion, providing global construction support to various government agencies.

Mr. Krapcha holds an A.S. in surveying from Pennsylvania State University and a B.S. and an M.S. in training and occupational education from the University of Southern Mississippi. He is a qualified Occupational Safety & Health Administration (OSHA) compliance inspector, a certified civil engineering technician, and a certified PMP®.

David Kaiser brings an extensive background in project management to his current role as a self-employed consultant and trainer assisting clients in getting control of their projects. Mr. Kaiser has held positions in marketing, quality assurance, business planning, and project management during his career at Xerox Corporation and the Eastman Kodak Company. In addition to managing projects to develop software applications, new equipment, and writable DVD media, he has experience in leading up-front requirements collection and definition efforts, including conducting focus groups in order to define new product requirements.

He has served as chapter vice president of professional development for the Project Management Institute and is an active member of a number of professional organizations.

Mr. Kaiser holds a degree in physics and an MBA and is a certified project management professional (PMP®).

ACKNOWLEDGEMENTS

This guide represents another major step in my relationship with ESI International. As the organization flourishes, I am grateful to have the opportunity to play an ongoing role. My thanks to ***J. LeRoy Ward, PMP®*** for his ongoing support (and for his glossary terms), and to ***Julie Zinn*** and ***Anne Feldman*** for their persistence in seeing this through to fruition.

A special thanks to ***Leonard Krapcha,*** a model professional and scheduling master, without whom significant issues in this text would have been left wanting.

And my thanks to ***David Kaiser,*** a long-time peer in distance learning and an ally in the battle for better schedules.

My gratitude also goes out to ***MaryBeth Pritchard,*** and ***Leonard*** and ***Joanne Pritchard,*** as well as ***J. Robert*** and ***Clara Hoon,*** who regularly support the efforts of Pritchard Management Associates.

As always, my deepest thanks go out to my students, who consistently challenge me to find new tools and new opportunities.

CHAPTER 1

PRECEDENCE DIAGRAMMING

Introduction

Although the fundamental practice of precedence diagramming has been applied for more than 30 years, relatively little literature about the subject is available. Project managers will find more information about the activity-on-arrow approach than the precedence diagramming approach in both the academic and the popular press. Although the activity-on-arrow approach worked well in the early days of modern project management, today it applies only to a handful of software tools and packages. The precedence diagramming method—the most common method in software packages—is far more flexible and easy to manage than the activity-on-arrow approach from both a visual and a team management perspective.

This guide will provide you with a clear understanding of how to interpret a precedence diagram, how to construct a precedence diagram, and how to use it to facilitate better schedules and more accurate sensitivity analyses.

Basics of Precedence Diagramming

The precedence diagram is designed to provide a clear perspective about which activities precede other activities. It is based on the notion that "first you dig the hole, and then you pour the foundation." It is simple and sequential. The challenge of using precedence diagramming in project management does not come with the basic practice. It involves the sheer volume of activities. As the number of activities woven into the project increases, it becomes more difficult to identify *all* the relationships and to assess their relative necessity.

The key to effective precedence diagramming is ensuring that you identify all activities and that you establish the relationships between them. This discussion examines the best and simplest practices of precedence diagramming. These practices make the precedence diagram not only the most popular schedule planning tool in modern project management software, but also the best tool for scheduling in a team environment.

What Is a Precedence Diagram?

A precedence diagram is a series of activities that are linked by arrows to reflect their precedential relationships. A precedence diagram, in its simplest form, looks something like this—

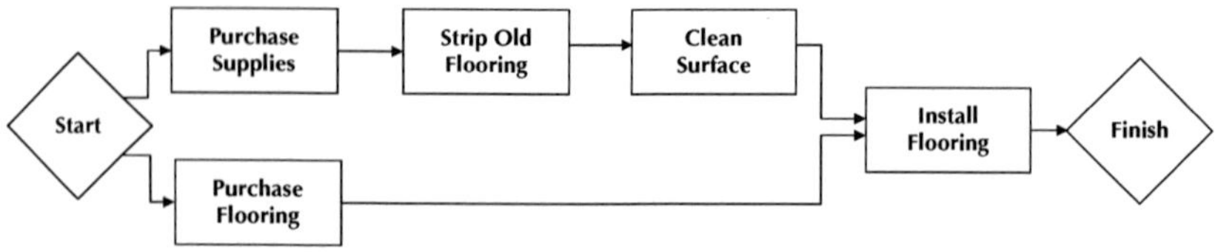

In the example provided here, the precedence diagram reflects very basic relationships. A person cannot strip the old flooring until the supplies have been purchased. The surface cannot be cleaned until the old flooring is stripped off. Each activity has a clear relationship with the next activity. That is the basic premise of the precedence diagram.

Description

A good, formal description of the precedence diagramming method (PDM) comes from the PMBOK® Guide[1] where it is described as *a network diagramming technique in which activities are represented by boxes. Activities are linked by precedence relationships to show the sequence in which the activities are to be performed.* In layman's terms, PDM takes each element of work, puts it in a box, and then identifies (with arrows), which boxes come before other boxes and which boxes come after other boxes.

One project management student had yet another description. He laughed about the concept, referring to PDM output as "spaghetti networks." He thought the abundance of lines criss-crossing the diagram made it impossible to interpret which activities preceded which other activities.

The above description is one of the primary reasons some project managers avoid precedence diagrams. They sense that the level of

"PMBOK" is a trademark of the Project Management Institute, Inc., which is registered in the United States and other nations.

effort involved in precedence diagram development and the potential for confusion from the diagram do not justify its use. They would rather work from a calendar or from a simple, time-scaled bar chart (Gantt). These individuals, however, fail to acknowledge the one aspect of the precedence diagram that rarely is taken into account. By virtue of the precedence relationships and the network perspective, precedence diagrams allow for and encourage highly sensitive analyses that cannot be developed as easily from the Gantt view.

Nature

The precedence diagram represents a linear progression of work. That does not mean, however, that the precedence diagram is time-scaled. As the opening example indicates, the purchase flooring and purchase supplies tasks both had the same preceding milestone, "Start." That does not mean that those two activities have the same duration or must occur at the same time. It *only* means that they have the same predecessor. Most precedence diagrams are not time-scaled and do not reflect the chronological relationships between activities. They only show the sequence of such activities.

It is worthwhile to note that precedence diagrams are included in the "logic diagram" family. The network actually reflects the logical sequence of work and the logic that went into determining that sequence. Logic, per se, may differ from individual to individual and from organization to organization. The precedence diagram inherently reflects the logic of its creator(s).

The precedence diagram does not show the relative magnitude of activities. Unless it is a time-scaled precedence diagram (discussed later), it is impossible to tell the relative duration of two activities by looking at the diagram. Nor is it possible to ascertain the number of resources assigned or the relative importance of the work. The diagram *does* illustrate the importance of an activity if it drives numerous other activities and if they rely on its output. Otherwise, there is no easy means to discern the importance of given activities from the precedence diagram perspective.

The precedence diagram also can reflect risk. Because it illustrates the number of paths that are occurring concurrently, it shows where the project manager's attention may be divided among competing priorities, and where the risk of management inattention may increase. Because it shows where multiple paths rely on a single output (or where multiple output converges to serve a single task), the precedence diagram can identify areas where the relationships between activities drive greater inherent risk.

Precedence diagrams tend to be somewhat large and unwieldy. The earlier example was a mere five activities and consumed a significant amount of space to be legible and workable. Had pertinent data such as the duration, start date, and finish date been included (many project management software packages include this data), only two or three tasks would have squeezed onto the page. A network of several hundred tasks may stretch across dozens of pages that (when generated on a normal printer) require extensive cutting, taping, and pasting. In more than one situation, project network diagrams may begin near the entrance of a room and stretch the length of more than two walls.

Uses

As you might imagine from that description, this is not a tool that is readily used for management presentations or reviews. It is not a tool that affords a quick and easy overview of information. It is a working tool, a construction tool. It is used to develop information and to clarify sequential relationships. As discussed later, it also is a tool used by management to bring the team together to establish the project schedule and the relationships that must exist within the team for the project to succeed.

The precedence diagram is best used as a working document. It is a standard of the project "war room." Corrections are made in pen and ink rather than fresh printouts. Very few project managers foster the notion that regular printouts of the precedence diagram are a good idea. Instead, corrections are made by hand, and updates are sporadic at best.

The tool is most useful in the nascent moments of the project, when team members work to establish their roles, responsibilities, and relationships. As examined in the closing pages of this text, the precedence diagram can serve as the cornerstone for those relationships and can provide inestimable value in terms of clarifying processes, relationships, and relative responsibilities.

Applications and Tools

Various software packages regularly mislabel the precedence diagram as a program evaluation and review technique (PERT) chart (a PERT chart is an activity-on-arrow diagram using three-data-point duration estimates). These software packages, however, have been instrumental in bringing the precedence diagram out of obscurity and into relative popularity among project managers. The precedence diagram rivals the indomitable Gantt chart as a primary or default perspective from which to view projects in some early versions of project management software. For instance, an old MS-DOS version of Computer Associates' *SuperProject®* initially opened to the precedence diagram view.

Although most software packages in the past 15 years have focused on the precedence diagram as a secondary perspective, that focus is changing. Some newer packages are working on a compromise between the popular Gantt view (bar charts) and the useful precedence diagram. One compromise is a Gantt perspective with dependencies, as illustrated here:

WBS	Task Name	Duration
1	**Web-We-Weave Project**	**39 days**
1.1	**Web Site Design**	**17 days**
1.1.1	**Design User Interface**	**8 days**
1.1.1.1	Determine site layout	4 days
1.1.1.2	Establish data link plan	4 days
1.1.1.3	Finalize list of desired functions	3 days
1.1.1.4	User Interface designed	0 days
1.1.2	**Design Server Setup**	**3 days**
1.1.2.1	Determine server memory requirements	0.5 days
1.1.2.2	Establish traffic estimates	0.5 days
1.1.2.3	Design access/security strategy	1 day
1.1.2.4	Design testing plan	3 days
1.1.2.5	Server designed	0 days
1.1.3	**Purchase and Integrate Server**	**6.5 days**
1.1.3.1	Finalize COTS software list	0.5 days
1.1.3.2	Meet with Procurement/Purchasing	0.5 days
1.1.3.3	Purchase server	0.5 days
1.1.3.4	Install and integrate server	2 days
1.1.4	**Develop Server Support Infrastructure**	**6 days**
1.1.4.1	Define any impact on network	2 days

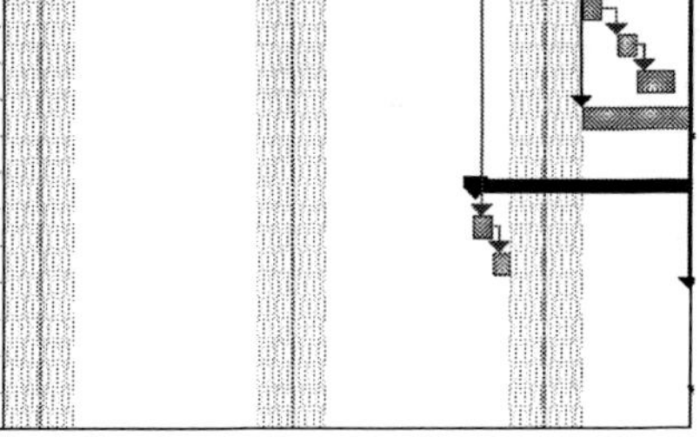

This type of time-scaled dependency diagram rapidly is becoming the default perspective in many popular software packages. Although it does capture the relationships among activities in much the same fashion as the conventional precedence diagram, it does not afford the clarity of those relationships as well as conventional PDM. As multiple tasks share predecessors and successors, the relationships rapidly become blurred and the originating (and terminating) points of the lines become difficult to discern.

In the end, precedence diagramming is best applied the old-fashioned way—by hand. By developing the precedence diagram from the ground up and then integrating that data into project management software, the project team gets greater visibility on the relationships, how they were established, and how they ultimately will work together.

Precedence Diagram History

The precedence diagram did not spring up overnight. It evolved from its simpler predecessor, the activity-on-arrow diagram—the "true" PERT chart. The activity-on-arrow perspective was epic in its simplicity. It presented every activity with a start and finish node and showed relationships between the activities by sharing those nodes. In the example below, Activity Start-1 "Purchase Supplies" precedes Activity 1-3 "Strip Old Flooring."

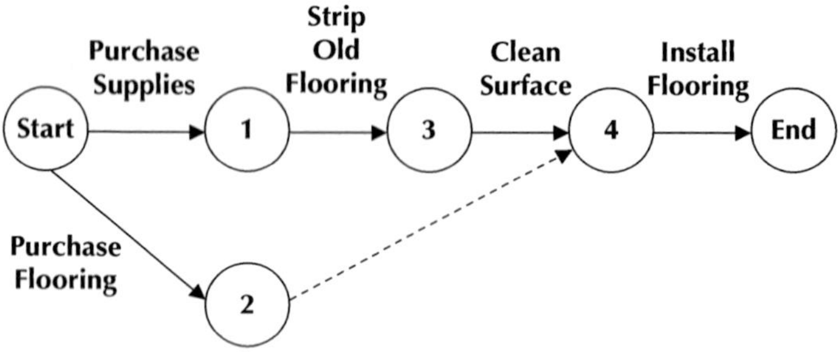

This perspective has some serious limitations, not the least of which is the use of "dummy" activities to show relationships, but no work (Activity 2-4). The preponderance of dummy activities and the highly integrative nature of the work in large-scale projects forced project management teams to seek other solutions.

The most significant steps forward came in the late 1950s and early 1960s, when the precedence diagram was developed. Different sources cite different origins for the precedence diagram. Some point to Stanford University as the birthplace of the precedence diagram,[2, 3] while others credit IBM for promoting the concept to prominence and credit Keith Crandall for ongoing promotion and evolution of the tool.[4]

In any case, the tool was born not only out of a need to reflect the increasingly complex relationships among activities, but also out of the need to reflect relationships of an ever-growing number of activities within projects. In addition, the ability to generate both conventional precedence diagrams as well as time-scaled precedence diagrams afforded a new dimension in information tracking and reporting.

Why Do Projects Need Precedence Diagrams?

Precedence diagrams are critical because they reflect both an understanding of the process by which the work is going to be performed and an understanding of the organizational relationships that exist. Reliance on conventional calendars, Gantt charts, and individual perceptions of how the work should be done leaves the project (and the organization) open to misinterpretation and mismanagement. Precedence diagrams limit the margin for error.

The PDM vs. The Gantt

The precedence diagramming method provides a dimension that the conventional bar chart or Gantt does not. A Gantt perspective often is generated based on organizational convention. "This is how we have always done the work, and this is how we will continue to do the work." That kind of argument is not entirely unreasonable. But it does not reflect best practice. And it does not reflect an organization's capacity to evolve. It limits the organization to conventional thinking.

Some organizations prefer conventional thinking. It hearkens back to a Dilbert© cartoon where the boss is instructing Dilbert to do his thinking "back inside the box" as he pushes him into his cubicle. It's not inherently wrong to promote the status quo.

The precedence diagram does, however, open new doors. It presents new opportunities and promotes innovative thinking. Reflect on the precedence diagram introduced earlier:

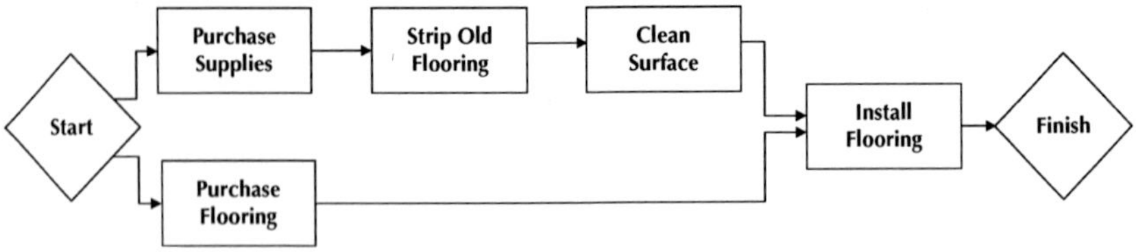

Are there other ways to approach the work? Are there relationships here that could be reconsidered? Certainly. One could consider purchasing only a floor scraper and leaving the other supply purchases until later to expedite the floor stripping process. One could strip away part of the old flooring; the surface on the west half of the room could be cleaned while the east half is being finished. An at-a-glance review of the precedence diagram opens a host of new opportunities. Granted, some of those opportunities might become evident from the Gantt perspective. It would be difficult, however, to discern what relationships must be modified as a result. The nature of the procedural changes becomes far more evident with the PDM.

The Gantt perspective has been (and may long be) the preferred perspective for presentations to customers and management. The PDM approach will never supplant it in those regards. And though the Gantt is familiar, easy to interpret, and easy to use, one should not assume that it is the solution to every problem.

The PDM evolved out of a need to reflect, respect, and sensitize analysis to more than a simple calendar. There was a clear need to understand and respect relationships. In recent years, project managers have built upon the foundation that was established by the precedence diagramming method with new and innovative ideas about how to make processes, systems, and projects more efficient. Most notable among these is the theory of constraints, a concept made popular by Eliyahu Goldratt's work, *The Critical Chain.*[5] Goldratt espouses the need to work from the foundation of a series of precedence relationships—a foundation established in PDM.

The Sensitivity of Relationships

Perhaps the most elegant aspect of precedence diagramming is its simple, fundamental expression of all tasks in terms of their relationship to other tasks. It does not focus on dates or on the nature of the work to be done. It focuses, wholly and clearly, on the relationships between tasks. Because every task is linked to other tasks, and because the tasks depend on each other, the precedence diagram focuses on the proclivity for one task to impact another.

Because every task in a precedence diagram affects another, the entire diagram serves as a massive case study in sensitivity analysis. If one changes the duration of a task early in the project, one can watch the effects of this change ripple through the entire effort. To understand the value of the precedence diagram as a sensitivity tool, it is important to understand its basic nature.

CHAPTER 2

PRECEDENCE DIAGRAM DEVELOPMENT

The precedence diagram is built from the building blocks of the project—the tasks. One must understand the nature of the work to be done at the micro level before developing a precedence diagram. A person cannot build an effective precedence diagram using a series of summary-level descriptions of the work to be done. To do so is to render the tool impotent.

Begin with tasks that are clearly delineated in a Gantt, a work breakdown structure (WBS), or a task list. Use those components to determine the workflow: which tasks come first, which come second, and which rely on the deliverables from other tasks before they can be performed. By establishing these sequential relationships, a person can build a logic network, a process, and a schedule. These same steps answer critical questions regarding how and why work must be done and processes that must be followed.

Integrating the WBS or Task List and the Precedence Diagram

Precedence diagram development begins with the WBS or task list. Note that the terms ***task list*** and ***WBS*** are not synonymous.

Some people argue that the WBS should not be included in a precedence diagramming discussion. These individuals argue (reasonably) that a WBS is a deliverables-oriented tool that cannot be used to outline tasks. They state that, at its lowest levels, the WBS outlines deliverables. These individuals should simply consider this precedence diagramming discussion as a review of the role of the task list and the precedence diagram.

Here, however, the lowest level of the WBS may be referred to as a work package or task.

Task lists and work packages provide a comprehensive list of the work to be done. Often tasks already are arranged in the WBS in the sequence in which they will be performed. Although that may expedite the precedence diagramming process, it does not replace it.

To develop the precedence diagram, one must begin with a start node. That node is crucial, both in practice and in the software packages. In either case, failure to include a start milestone can make it very difficult to assess the overall impact to the project when the start date is delayed or slipped. By creating a common starting point, one can examine what will happen if the start date is modified without changing the characteristics or qualities of the multiple tasks that occur at the project's outset. It anchors the rest of the project and often helps define the way work will be done later in the project.

Although a person may be tempted to use a common beginning task (such as "host kickoff meeting") as the start node, such a task is not appropriate as the start node. The opportunity to do work concurrently with the kickoff meeting or the chance to apply lag or lead time from the start node may be lost if the task becomes the node. Start should be a milestone, an activity of zero duration.

All project tasks must be placed in sequential order after the start node. And each task must have a predecessor and a successor (even if they are just the start node and the finish node, respectively). This simple process involves an analysis of each task: "What is the input," "What is the process," "What are the constraints (resource or otherwise)?", and "What is the output?" By asking those basic questions, one can determine relationships among the activities. These questions seem simple enough, but in many organizations, the seemingly mandatory relationships that exist between tasks are merely organizational convention, the status quo. Part of PDM is ensuring that the project manager has looked at some alternatives to conventional ways of doing business.

The Logic

Most tasks are connected by ***mandatory dependencies*** or ***hard logic.*** The following is an example of mandatory dependencies or hard logic: a person cannot go for a swim until the pool has been filled with water.

Most precedence diagrams are built on a foundation of hard logic dependencies. One establishes the relationships based on the laws of nature and physics. Although many organizations envision their activities as rooted in hard logic, the relationships are not actually mandatory.

Some of the best evidence of the kinds of conventions that are meant to be broken can be found in the San Diego Building Industry Association's landmark video, *The Four-Hour House.*[6] In the video, many normal practices of home construction are turned upside down as the organization works to set a world record for home construction. Think about some fundamental tasks associated with home construction. They might look (in small measure) like this—

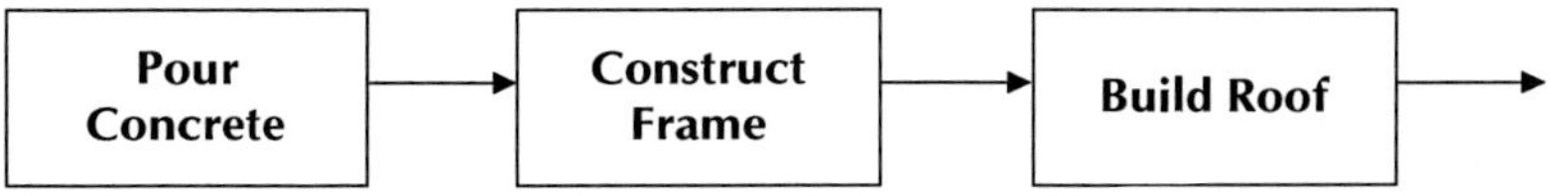

The above tasks appear to be mandatory dependencies. A person cannot start constructing a frame until there is a foundation to put it on.

These three activities, however, were performed concurrently in the world-record effort in San Diego. As the concrete was being poured, the frame was being constructed in another on-site location. At the same time, the roof was under construction elsewhere on the site. These would be parallel—not serial—tasks on the precedence diagram. Why? Because hard logic does not connect them; soft logic does.

Soft logic embodies more precedence relationships than most project managers acknowledge (or are aware of). ***Soft logic*** is precedence logic that is dictated by convention or preference—not the laws of nature or physics. In many cases, soft logic is mistaken for hard logic because the conventions are so well entrenched in traditional thinking. For example, most builders would never consider constructing the frame of a home while the foundation concrete is still being poured. But the sequence of "pour foundation" then "construct frame" is not dictated by hard logic. It is dictated by soft logic. Convention, not physics, drives the relationship in most environments.

In many environments, soft logic is used to reflect resource constraints rather than mandatory constraints. In others, it simply reflects convention. Either way, it reflects the lion's share of relationships. Sometimes it is done out of common sense or safety. Researchers at Fort

Detrick, Maryland do extensive work with infectious disease. After they complete such work, they decontaminate, then depart the work area. Theoretically, they could walk past the decontamination areas, leave, come back, and go through the decontamination process later. They never would. Why? Because soft logic preserves and protects the public's health and welfare. Soft logic does not imply superfluous action. It warrants serious consideration. Soft logic is borne out of practice, habit, convention, resource allocation, and preference.

Preferential logic often is a subset of soft logic. Preferential logic involves performing tasks a particular way because you—or the customer, or management—prefers it to be done a certain way. Imagine if the contractor building a home said "I'm going to build the roof while we are pouring the concrete." The owner of the home might become concerned about the quality of the work, the nature of the approach, and the sanity of the contractor. The customer may contest the contractor's preference and say, "I want you to pour the slab, then build the frame. *Then, and only then,* build the roof." It does not have to be done that way. But the customer prefers it to be done that way. It is preferential logic.

A person does not need to invest a lot of time determining whether tasks are connected using hard or soft logic. A person may, however, want to keep this concept in mind as he or she is searching for alternative approaches and means to expedite the work. By acknowledging which relationships are "hard" and which are "soft," people may find new methods that will serve themselves and their organizations better.

Establishing the Fundamental Relationships

Now that the differences between hard, soft, and preferential logic have been defined, it is time to examine basic relationships and how they are established in most projects.

Most logic is preordained. And most logical relationships are defined as finish-start—even though many projects would be better served by other relationships made available through PDM. Those other relationships are finish-finish, start-start, and the somewhat esoteric start-finish. And all these relationships can be further modified with the use of lag and lead time. The most popular relationship, however, is the basic finish-start relationship. And it probably always will be.

The Basics of the Finish-Start Relationship

The finish-start (FS) relationship is grounded in the idea that the deliverables from one task will serve as the input to another. That is why workers perform tasks. Ultimately, the deliverables from all the tasks will weave together to form a finished product that is capable of meeting the customer's needs. In a finish-start relationship, one assumes that the start of the successor activity depends upon completion of its predecessor. For this discussion (and for most academic precedence relationships discussions) the two activities in the relationship will be described as *i* and *j*.

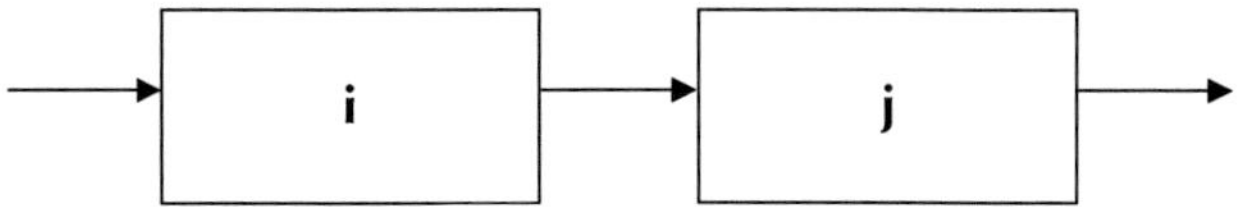

In the classic examples, *i* must finish before *j* can start. The design documents must be finished before development can begin. The bridge must be constructed before toll collections can start. After the semifinal matches are complete, the finals can begin. Finish-start relationships characterize many day-to-day activities.

In determining if a relationship should be a finish-start relationship, the project manager or team member should ask the question "Am I required to wait until *i* is finished before *j* can start?" It is important to know the answer to that question. In many instances, convention forces people to use finish-start relationships unnecessarily (for example, resource limitations force people into soft logic dependencies). In just as many instances, the relationship must be modified to account for any lag or lead time that might need to be introduced into the relationship.

Introducing Lag and Lead Time

In many situations, the relationships between activities must be modified to account for the passage of time or to account for the performer's capacity to get a head start on the successor. Lag and lead allow for those considerations. Lag time is defined in a variety of ways. One text refers to it as "an offset from an activity to its successor."[7] Another describes it as a "modification of the logical relationship that directs a delay in the successor task." [8] In essence, lag is "waiting time." In most situations, it is better for the lag between activities to be negligible, because it extends the total duration of the project if it is on the critical path. (This issue will be discussed in more detail later.)

Lag often reflects the reality of a situation. If a person paints the room, he or she must wait for the paint to dry. If a person orders a system, he or she must wait for the processing system to churn through its machinations. If a person roasts a turkey, he or she must wait for the turkey to cool before carving it. Lag is part of day-to-day life. It consumes no resources. If the task consumes personnel resources, the resources can work on other tasks during the lag time. If the task uses material resources, those resources can be deployed elsewhere. Lag simply is a window of imposed time in the relationship.

It is important to acknowledge that lag time is, in some cases, radically different from working time. Because it is "waiting time," it may not need to share the "working clock" with the rest of the precedence diagram. Suppose a person has a project with just two tasks: "Paint Room" and "Inspect Work." The room will be painted in a heavy, oil-based enamel paint that will take 24 hours to dry. The painting effort will take about 8 hours. Conventionally, the relationship might be displayed as—

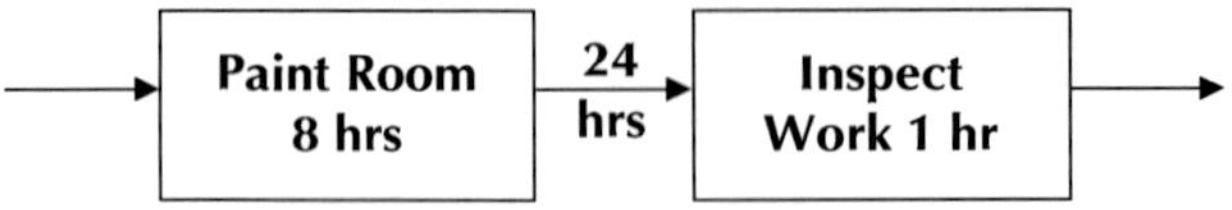

That communicates the message that at least 24 hours must pass before the work can be inspected. But it also may skew the message. Painting the room is an 8-hour effort. Consider the conditions of those 8 hours. They must be during working hours (whenever those may be). If the paint room task were a 16-hour effort, it would take 2 days. The imposed lag between i and j is 24 hours. Is that 3 days? No!

It is only a day. It is a different type of time. It is elapsed time—not working time.

This is an important distinction because not all lag time is elapsed. In cases where the lag is "waiting time" for an organizational process or cycle, lag may be counted as working time in business days or hours.

Therefore, before people can begin calculating a network or assessing their ability to meet a schedule, they must first ascertain what kind of time they are dealing with. This is most evident when examining lag between activities.

When can the room be inspected in the example below, if the project starts Monday at 8 a.m. and the workday is 8 a.m. to 5 p.m. (with an hour for lunch). Following the diagram, Monday is the day to paint. The room will dry from 5 p.m. Monday to 5 p.m. Tuesday. Inspection can begin Wednesday morning at 8 a.m.

In classes, students argue that there is no sense in waiting an extra day to inspect the room. Students challenge that, "The last hour of room painting was probably clean-up time anyway! This could be done and inspected by close of business on Tuesday." That is a fair and reasonable argument. However, to make it work in a precedence diagram, the basic structure of the work must be reconsidered.

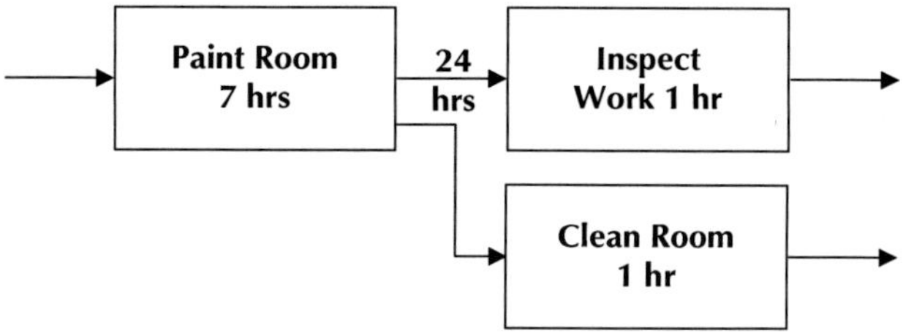

Note that the nature of the work has not changed because of the lag. Lag has clarified the work process, but the relationships remain intact. And people do not necessarily need to revise the task list or WBS every time they build a precedence diagram. In many cases, however, a thorough and critical review of the relationships in the network diagram will lead to changes in the definition of the work to be done.

In some cases, the evaluation of lag time (and how to make best use of it) will lead to such discussions.

The opposite of lag time is lead time. ***Lead time*** is applied when a task does not need to be complete before the next task starts, but it does need to be near completion. Many organizations use lead time to make their processes as user friendly as possible. For example, some organizations begin the ordering process several days before the sales cycle ends. Even though contracts have not been signed, the organization will begin placing orders, staging equipment, and moving resources in preparation for the initiation of work.

Using the earlier example of a room-painting project, lead time can be used to acknowledge the physical realities of the situation:

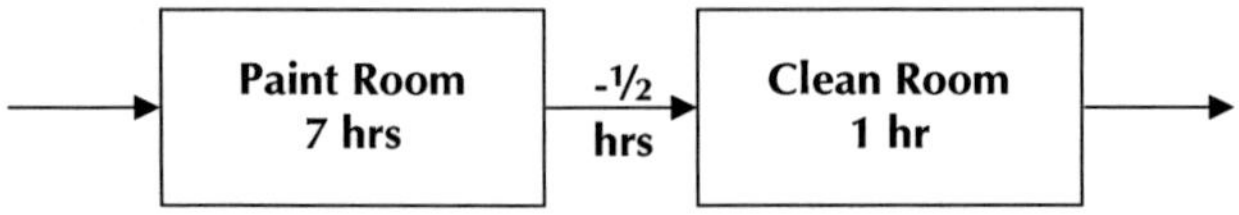

Lead time is expressed in the same manner as lag time. It is calculated along the line of the relationship. But rather than adding time between the activities, it is expressed as a negative number. In this instance, the lead time indicates that those responsible for cleaning the room can begin to work a half hour before the room-painting work is complete. In this scenario, it is easy to envision how lead time would be implemented. As the painters complete the final corners of the room, the cleaners can begin picking up loose material and throwing out trash in another area of the room. Lead time shows that certain tasks are completed in degrees—not all at once. It also acknowledges that the relationship between the completion of *i* and the start of *j* does not rely on deliverables alone.

Calculating the Network Diagram

All the information ultimately is integrated into the network diagram. The precedence diagram is built on the collective relationships that exist among the tasks. Organized properly, they present the flow of the work to be performed and establish the baseline schedule for that work. Although most modern project management software packages can make the calculations, it is vital to understand the roots of those calculations. In the discussion that follows, the diagrams will be built incrementally to allow for easy display. It is important to recognize that under normal conditions, the logical relationships are established clearly across the entire network *before* the calculations are applied. The network under review in this sample follows.

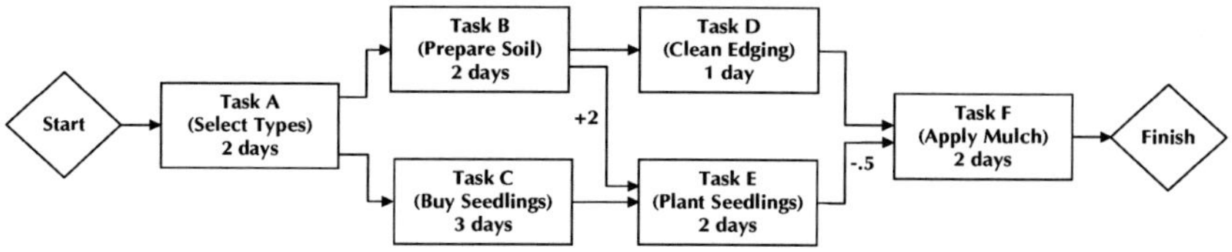

The network takes advantage of the lag and lead times and all types of logic. Soft logic guides the team to prepare the soil after selecting the types of seedlings to plant. In most environments, the two could, technically, be done in parallel. But they are not done in parallel because people prefer to do it the other way (preferential logic) or they cannot do the tasks in parallel due to resource constraints. Hard logic is reflected in the relationship between buying the seedlings and planting them. People cannot plant materials they do not have. Lag exists between the soil preparation time and the planting time because some fertilizers must "cure" before plants are introduced. No one needs to watch over the curing process. The lag identifies waiting time associated with the relationship. A half day of lead time exists between the planting and mulching activities. That means people can start mulching a half day before the planting activity is finished.

Take note of the previous paragraph. It reflects the thinking that went into this network diagram. It explains the logic of the relationships. The logic of one planner may differ radically from that of another. The logic should be firmly entrenched before the calculations are done.

The Forward Pass

Put a start milestone at the beginning of the network diagram, and assign a value of Day 0 to it. This can apply whether a person is using either of two popular calculation techniques: the 24-hour clock and the 8-hour clock. The term ***24-hour clock*** means that a given day starts at 8 a.m. and ends at 7:59 a.m. the following day. The term ***8-hour clock*** means that a given day begins (for instance) at 8 a.m. and ends at 5 p.m. the same day, including 1 hour for lunch. Both approaches may assign a value of zero to the start milestone, although the Day 0 start is more common with the 24-hour clock.

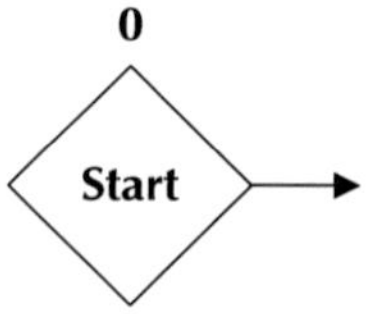

The next several pages focus on a forward pass that will be conducted through the network. The forward pass will calculate the earliest time each activity may begin (early start) and the earliest time each activity may finish (early finish) based on network constraints. The forward pass will be calculated using the 24-hour clock.

Let's look at a simple project to prepare and plant a bed of tomatoes. In this effort, the project is to determine the correct crops, prepare the beds, and plant the tomatoes. Assume that all the basic gardening equipment and supplies are on hand. You, the project manager, own the beds (250' x 250') and have worked in them before. Note the importance of clarifying the assumptions before networking. If the project goal were simply a tomato bed preparation project, some people would argue that the first activities should involve site survey, materials procurement, customer reviews, and a host of other planning activities. From the first activity, the network diagram clarifies precisely what work is being done and what processes will be applied.

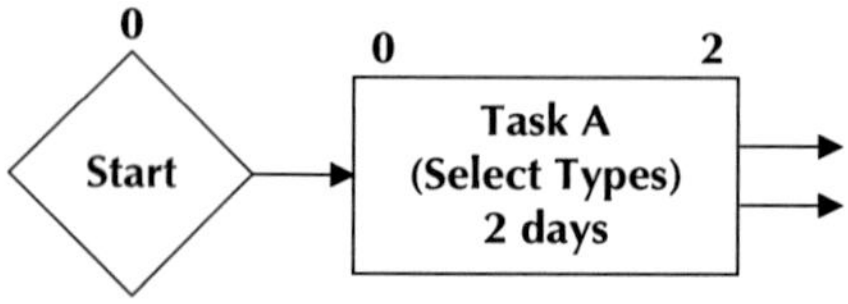

Task A begins on Day 0 and continues through all of Day 1. It ends at 8 a.m. on Day 2. This process is advantageous because it allows for simple calculations throughout the network. The earliest an activity can finish (early finish (EF)) always becomes the earliest the next activity can start (early start (ES)). The ES of task A, for example, is driven by the start milestone. Calculate the early finish of task A by adding the duration of the task to the task's early start. The first task in the network has an early start on Day 0. The early start of zero (0), plus the duration of two (2), totals two (2). That becomes the earliest time this activity can finish, based on the precedence diagram.

The next two activities make the project more complex and more interesting.

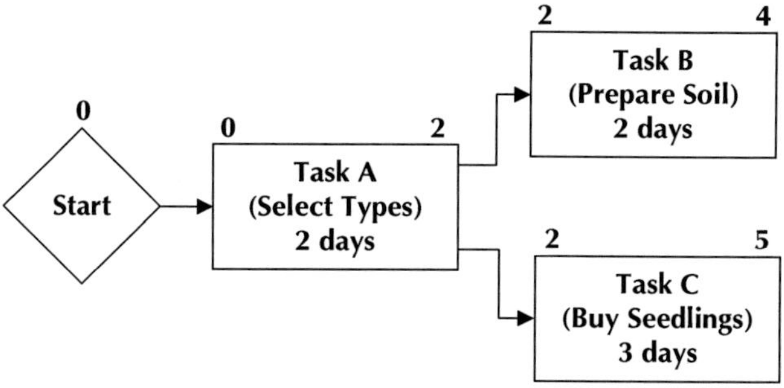

The diagram indicates that the ES for tasks B and C is the same as the early finish of their common predecessor. Task B begins at 8 a.m. on Day 2 and continues through all of Days 2 and 3, ending at 7:59 a.m. on Day 4. Task C, similarly, begins at 8 a.m. on Day 2, with work being performed on Days 2, 3, and 4 (with the early finish at 7:59 a.m. on Day 5).

The basic mathematical expression is—

$$ESj = EFi + FSij$$

(It is important to note that when an activity has multiple predecessors, the latest of the $EFi + FSij$ is applied in the formula.)

This finish-start relationship indicates that the only thing that must happen before anyone prepares the soil is the selection of the types of tomatoes to plant. Similarly, the type selection process is the only thing that must happen before buying the seedlings.

As the network evolves and becomes progressively more complex, the math remains simple. It is a function of basic carryovers and addition from tasks to successors.

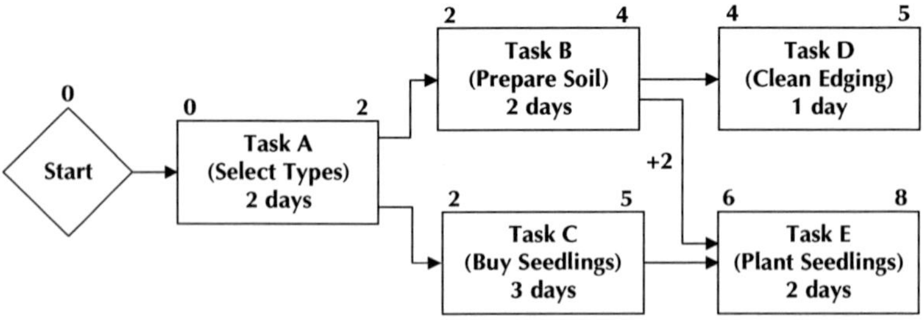

Here, a number of assumptions are clear. First, the soil must "cure" or settle for at least 2 days after preparation. This accounts for the 2 days of lag time assigned on the FS relationship between task B and task E. Also, it is evident that the seedlings cannot be planted until they have been purchased. The relationship between tasks B and D has no lag time. The soil does not have to cure before the edging bricks are cleaned for the spring season. The B-to-D relationship is finish-start with no lag. B finishes at 7:59 a.m. on Day 4. And task D begins at 8 a.m. Task D continues through 7:59 a.m. the following day. It is only a 1-day activity. Task E relies on *both* tasks B and C. Task C will be complete and then E can start, *unless* B has not finished. Note that the finish-start relationship, with its 2 days of lag, means that task E can begin 48 hours after the finish of task B. (In this instance, some fertilizers require modest curing time to avoid root damage to young seedlings.) Although initially it would have appeared that the purchasing activity (task C) would drive the planting activity (task E), that is not the case. Soil preparation (and the subsequent curing time) determines the early start of the seedling planting.

The Gantt equivalent of the network diagram on the previous page is presented below:

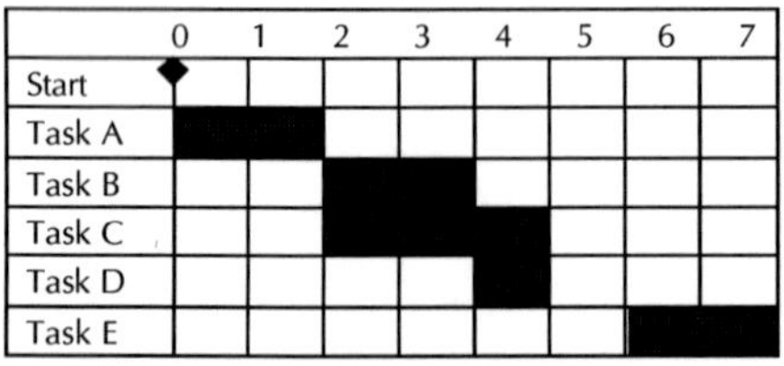

Note that the Gantt does not reflect relationships and does not provide the critical information that task E is driven by task B—not task C or task D. The precedence diagram illustrates those relationships clearly and defines how they are established.

Thus far, the network has been calculated (using the 24-hour clock) applying FS relationships and some lag time. The other key aspect applied in many basic network diagrams is lead time.

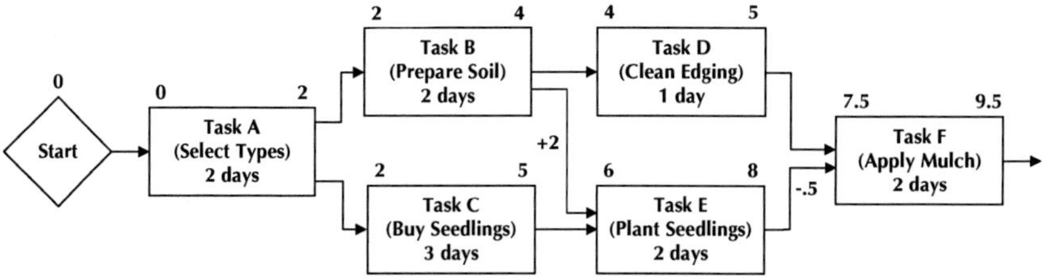

In this scenario, mulch application cannot begin until the edging is cleaned thoroughly. Mulch application also is in a finish-start relationship with the planting task. One may begin to apply mulch one-half day before the last seedling is planted. The planned completion time of the seedling planting task drives the project. It will determine the start time for mulch application. The arrangement, however, allows one to start applying mulch before the last seedling is planted. Lead time affords people a half day of work on mulch while planting continues elsewhere in the tomato patch.

This means that one may begin applying mulch halfway through the workday on Day 7.

Assuming that task F is the final task in the project, the project now has a total duration. If everything goes as planned, the project will be complete in 9.5 days. If the network is used to establish the total project duration, the entire effort will be complete 9.5 days after it begins.

The mathematical expressions for the calculations of the 24-hour clock are—

$$ESi + DURi = EFi$$

$$EFi + FSij = ESj$$

As long as there is an understanding that the early start of *j* always will be the highest number generated by the predecessors, the math of this approach is relatively simple.

Alternative Calculation of the Forward Pass

An alternative approach to calculating the network can be used, although the final outcome will be the same. The previous approach assumed a 24-hour clock to calculate activity to activity. The alternative uses the classic 8-hour workday.

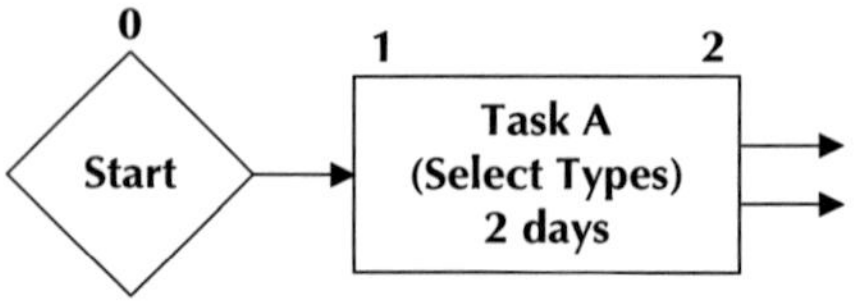

When using the 8-hour day approach, the first task begins on Day 1 rather than Day 0. Day 1 begins at 8 a.m. and continues through the 5 p.m. whistle. It is a 2-day task, and as is evident from the diagram, task A consumes Day 1 and Day 2.

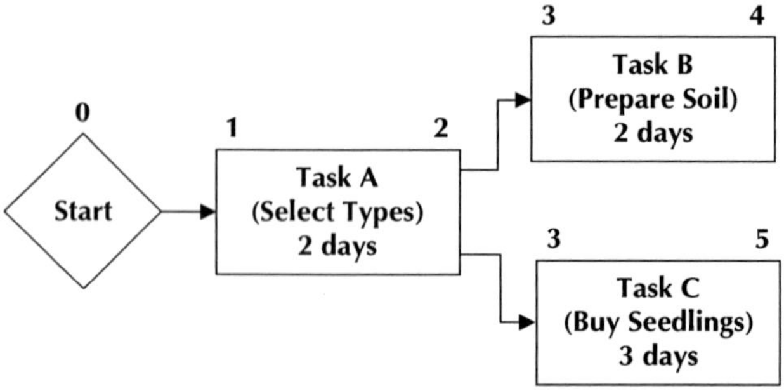

Note the transition to the first pair of tasks. Rather than simply carrying over the early finish of task A, one day is added. The mathematical expression is—

$$ESj = EFi + 1 + FSij$$

The math is slightly more complicated than it was with the 24-hour clock. Each finish-start relationship must have a day added to it, whether or not any lag or lead is applied.

The basic duration calculations change as well. Task B begins the morning of Day 3 and ends the close of business on Day 4. The early start of the task begins on Day 3. To calculate the end date, the scheduler must add the duration of the activity and subtract one. Thus, task C begins on Day 3. Three plus three equals six (the early start plus the duration). Subtract one, and it becomes evident that task C will be complete on Day 5. The mathematical expression to calculate duration becomes—

$$EFi = ESi + DURi - 1$$

Because every relationship and every task forces the "plus-one, minus-one" cycle, many practitioners have migrated to the 24-hour clock. However, this approach affords a very clear and understandable perspective about when activities are to begin and end.

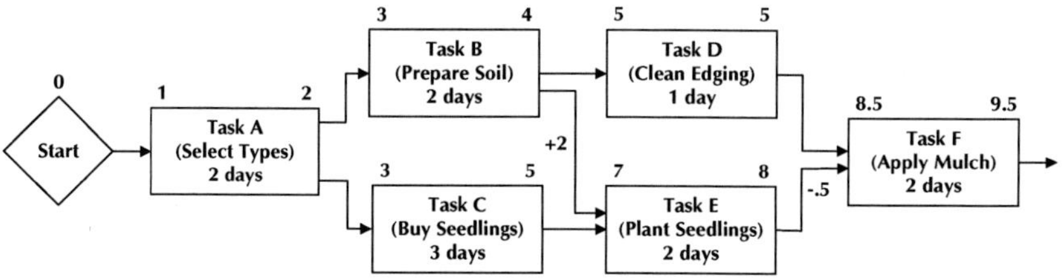

The project's end date remains unchanged. It will still be done in 9.5 days. However, the calculations look different and the information is conveyed differently.

Which Approach Is More Effective in the Forward Pass?

A person's objectives for the process largely determine the approach he or she selects. If a person is using hand calculations as a temporary stopgap until the information is loaded into a software package, the 24-hour clock is a far quicker, easier way to calculate information that is embedded in the relationships. It is quick, effective, and easy to calculate and recalculate.

If, however, the forward pass will be generated in a hand-crafted diagram to be used on an ongoing basis, the "8-hour clock" or "plus-one, minus-one" approach probably is more effective. Although the calculations are more arduous, the outcome is easier to understand and easier for team members to work with.

Although the forward pass provides most project managers with the information they need to manage on a day-to-day basis (in terms of schedule), it does not provide the full depth of information that precedence diagramming provides. Much of that in-depth information comes from a review of the network from a backward pass.

The Backward Pass

The backward pass provides a great deal of insight in terms of how projects can be managed. It provides information about free time driven by the network (known conventionally as "float"). It allows project managers to work toward more balance within the schedules and toward an understanding of different ways to approach the work.

As with the forward pass, the easiest way to calculate the backward pass is with the 24-hour clock. At the end of both the forward and backward pass discussions on network analysis, there will be a review of how to conduct the same effort using the 8-hour clock approach.

To calculate the backward pass, the scheduler begins at the finish milestone rather than the start milestone.

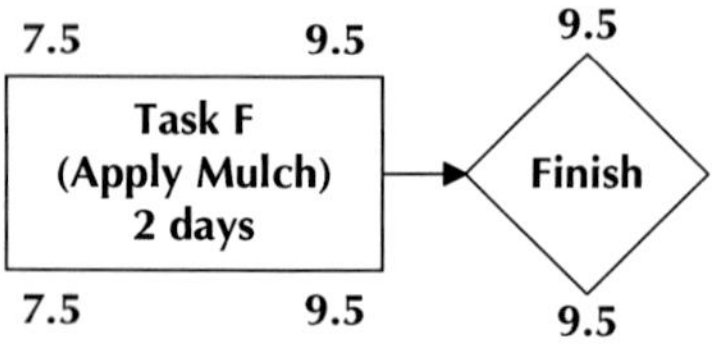

The information above shows that the project will take 9.5 days to complete. To complete the project on time, the mulch-application task must be completed 9.5 days into the project, at latest. To determine the latest time the mulch-application task can start (and still get the project done on time), subtract the duration from the 9.5-day late finish (LF) of the tasks. Reduce the 9.5-day duration by 2 days. The late start time is Day 7.5.

The first, and most obvious, conclusion is that the early start and the late start are identical. That is an important indicator on any task. It means that it has no slack, and that even the slightest delay on that task will drive a delay in the project. The task is ***critical.*** The basic definitions of the terms ***early start*** (the earliest a task can start based on the network logic) and ***late start (LS)*** (the latest a task can start without driving a delay) clarify that if ES and LS are the same, then the activity is critical. The task is a driving force in the schedule.

When stepping back one more pair of tasks, the difference in the two paths becomes evident. Across the bottom, task E clearly is showing many of the same traits as task F. It has no slack. It allows for no free time. The late start is the same as the early start. The late finish is the same as the early finish.

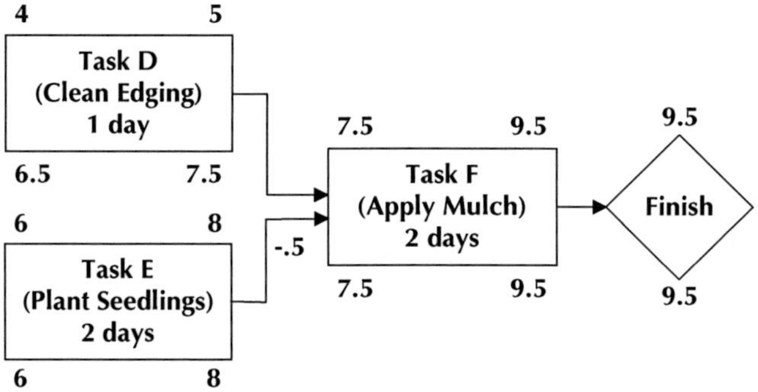

Working backward through the network, the FS relationship is subtracted from the late start of the successor task to establish the late finish of the previous task. It is expressed mathematically as—

$$LFi = LSj - FSij$$

In the example provided, the logic goes from a late start (LSj) of 7.5 days to an early finish (EFi) of 8 days. The half-day of lead time (expressed as a negative because it is lead, rather than lag) is a negative subtracted from 7.5; 7.5 minus negative .5 equals 8.

It is relatively simple to calculate the late start and the late finish on the top path. As with the other 24-hour clock example, the late start of the task carries directly back to the late finish. The late finish of task D, clean edging, is 7.5 days into the task. That means that the edge-cleaning activity may finish as late as halfway through the seventh day without negatively affecting the remainder of the project. It is critical for project managers to know how late they can afford to be.

In the example, it is equally important to note the difference between the late finish and the early finish. If this task is completed as early as possible, it will be done by Day 5. If it is completed as late as possible, it will be done halfway through Day 7. There is a 2.5-day difference. That is 2.5 days of total float (TF) or total slack. ***Total slack*** means that the 2.5 days span the path in the network. Those 2.5 days are crucial. Those days are something that project managers, who frequently complain about their management authority, actually can manage. Resources can be leveled without damaging the overall project duration during those days, and gaps in resource allocation can be identified so underused team members can be applied to other activities. Project managers can accommodate their desire to modify schedules and adjust resource allocations to take full advantage of the way the network is established.

Working backward through the network, if the task finishes halfway through Day 7, a full day of work would drive it to a late start of halfway through Day 6. Because the calculations parallel one another, total float can be calculated either of two ways:

$$TF = LFi - EFi \text{ or}$$
$$TF = LSi - ESi$$

The results always will be the same. In the example provided above, the result of either approach is still 2.5. There is a 2.5-day difference. This means that the project manager has 2.5 days to reallocate resources, modify plans, change approaches, or provide team members with needed schedule relief. It is 2.5 days to manage.

Thus far, the math is relatively simple. It becomes more complicated as the remaining activities are calculated.

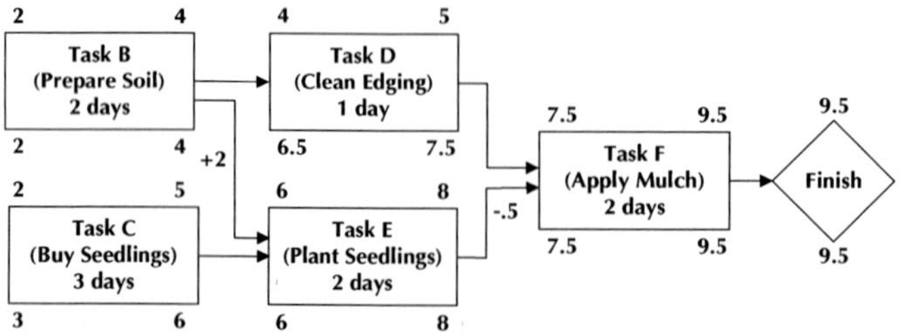

Work across the bottom first. The latest task C can finish is the morning of Day 6. The entire project will be delayed if task C finishes any later. The late finish for the task is 1 day later than the early finish for the same task. That means the task either can have a 1-day overrun or the resource can have a day off without affecting the network as a whole. Because task C has a day of total float, it is clearly not on the critical path.

To establish the late start of task B, the lag time associated with the task must be taken into account. The latest task E can start is Day 6. With that late start, the 2 days for the soil to cure still must be considered. The late finish of "prepare soil" is Day 4. The calculation in this instance (as before) subtracts out the time applied on the FS relationship. In this case, the time applied on the path is lag rather than lead. Therefore, when subtracting a positive number, the outcome is a late finish that is earlier than the late start of the successor. In simpler terms, if you must wait for something when conducting the forward pass, you must wait for it when conducting the backward pass. Going forward you add it. Going backward you subtract it.

$$LFi = LSj - FSij$$

In this instance, that calculates out as—

4 (the late finish of task B) =
6 (the late start of E) – 2 (the lag on the FS relationship)

The late finish for the 4-day task mirrors the early finish. If the late finish and the early finish are the same, the task is critical. Any delay here will prompt a delay in the project as a whole.

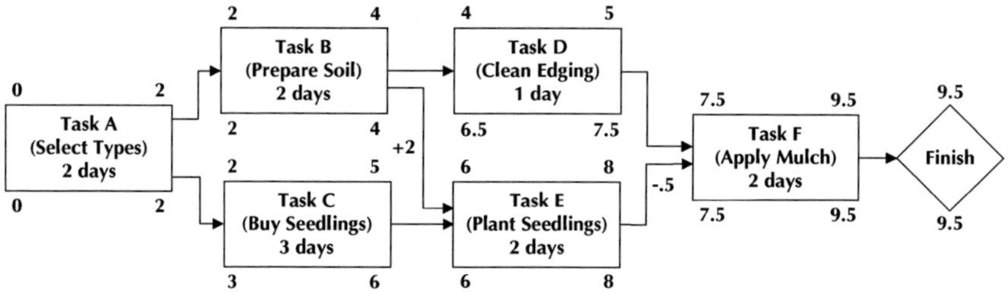

Adding in the last activity opens the door to complete the critical path calculation by defining which path goes from beginning to end with no slack or float. Beginning with task A, the critical path incorporates tasks A, B, E, and F. None of those tasks have total float.

Alternative Calculation of the Backward Pass

As with the forward pass, the backward pass also can be calculated using the "plus-one, minus-one" approach. When calculating the backward pass, the formulas are inverted, so the numbers are subtracted between tasks, rather than added.

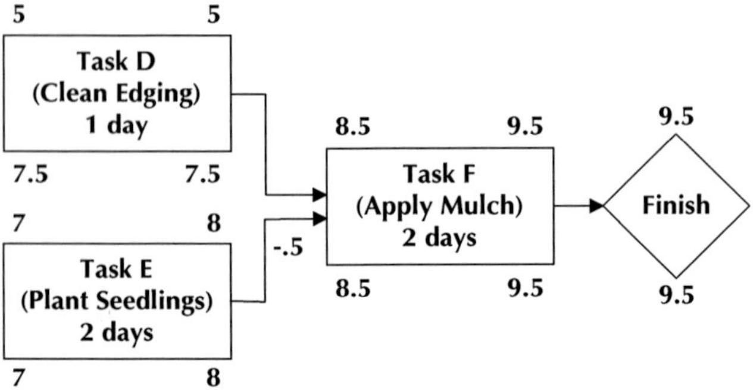

This scenario points to one shortcoming with the "plus-one, minus-one" approach. The "plus-one, minus-one" approach works perfectly and communicates information more clearly than the carryover approach as long as the time scale is in full days or full weeks. But the introduction of half-days and/or half-weeks makes this approach significantly more difficult to follow than the carryover approach. The edging activity still begins halfway through Day 7 for task D. However, it actually ends halfway through Day 8. The way the information is communicated in this approach makes it appear almost instantaneous. Instead, what the network diagram says is that "This task begins at the beginning of Day 7.5 and ends at the end of Day 7.5." It does not accommodate the 24-hour clock. Therefore, modest confusion may occur when anything except full days is accounted for.

The good news is that the total float or total slack calculations remain the same.

$$TF = LF - EF$$

$$TF = LS - ES$$

No adjustment is required because of the change in technique. As for the basic backward pass calculations in this approach, the late finish and late start are calculated as follows—

$$LSi = LFi - DURi + 1$$

The calculations from task to task also take the earlier formulas and work them in reverse.

$$LFi = LSj - FSij - 1$$

This allows for interpretation of the tasks from the 8-hour-clock perspective rather than the 24-hour clock. But, as the example above shows, it can lead to some modest confusion when the duration (DUR) of an activity spans half days rather than whole days.

Working the entire network through the backward pass ultimately looks like this—

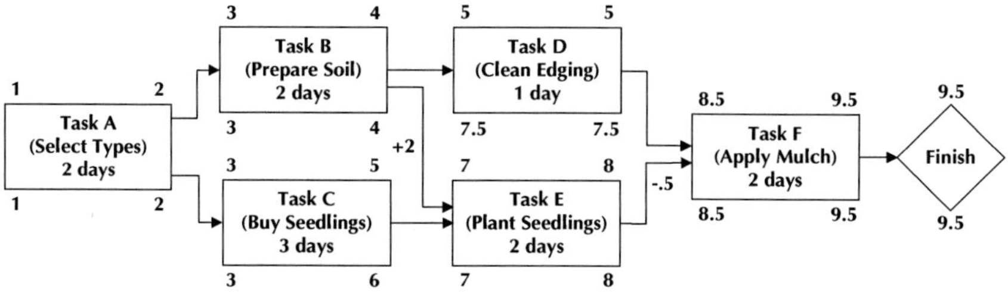

Task durations have not changed. The only element that has changed is the perspective that days begin at 8 a.m. and end at 5 p.m. The only confusion this introduces is with tasks that begin halfway through the day, because there is no such thing as 8 a.m. on Day 7.5. It is up to the project manager to interpret and clarify for those who might be confused.

Which Approach Is More Effective in the Backward Pass?

The approach a person selects is determined largely by his or her objectives. Many organizations are satisfied with a forward pass. They do not see a need for the additional managerial information provided by the backward pass. However, if the clarity of the information provided by the backward pass is critical to teach members, use the 24-hour, or carryover, approach.

The calculations involved in conducting a backward pass using the 8-hour clock, "plus-one, minus-one" approach tend to confuse people.

As such, some project managers prefer the 24-hour clock any time a backward pass will be part of the consideration. It is easier to calculate and easier to make the transitions across relationships, particularly when lag and/or lead are applied.

Calculations will be provided in the context of the 24-hour clock for the remainder of this PDM discussion.

Total Float vs. Free Float

Total float is driven by the difference between the late finish and early finish of an activity (or by the late start and early start). It is a function of the whole network or of a path within the network.

Total float identifies how much an activity can be delayed without potentially driving a change in the end date of the project. Total float identifies the additional duration that can be incurred without creating an additional critical path. Although it is calculated on an activity-by-activity basis, total float is shared across activities in a path. If it is consumed in the first activity, it will vanish for the second. At one time, total float also was referred to as ***shared float.*** As such, total float provides insight about the amount of uncommitted time shared by a series of activities in a path.

Free float is a far more sensitive measure than total float. ***Free float*** is a function of a given task and its nearest successor activity. For example, project managers often are assigned team members for a limited amount of time. Suppose a team member (hereafter referred to as "Bob") is waiting for another team member (hereafter referred to as "Clara") to complete her task before he can begin. For this analysis, Bob and Clara's tasks are not on the critical path. If Clara is delayed by a single day, it means that Bob cannot begin his activities. The project is not delayed, but Bob's performance is hampered by his inability to start work without Clara's deliverables. There is no free float in this scenario. Bob's late start will not hamper the overall project, but it may be detrimental to his ability to get his work done in a timely fashion or to do it without creating a conflict with other work. Clara has no free float. If she delays by as much as a day, Bob's work will start late. Their activities on the network might look like this—

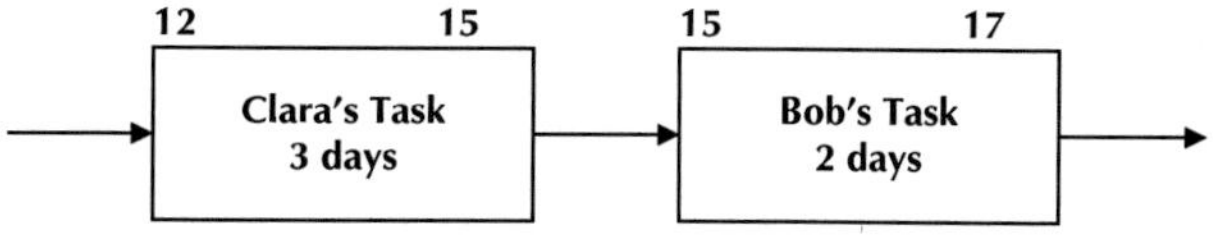

That is the nature of free float. It exists only when a task will not have any influence on its successors if it is delayed. Suppose that Bob and Clara's tasks also were connected to Mary Beth's:

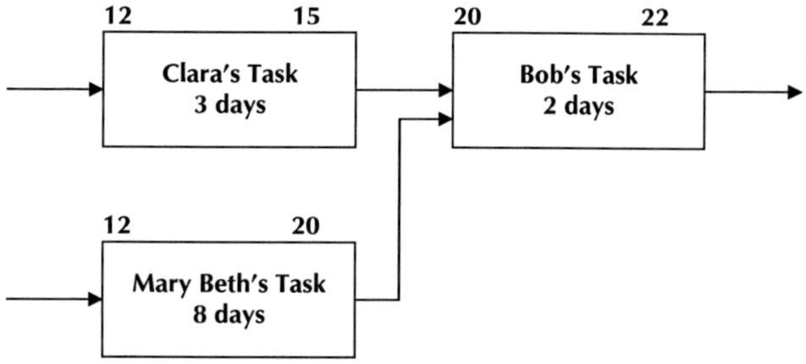

The question that surfaces once again is "What happens if Clara's task is delayed?" In this scenario, a delay on Clara's part will not affect Bob at all. In fact, she can be as much as 5 days late without forcing Bob to reconsider his schedule. There are 5 days of free float in which her task will not influence the following task.

What changed? Mary Beth now is driving Bob's schedule. Clara has free time to work on other tasks, or she can complete her task in a timely fashion. Either way, she has free float. To examine this further, suppose that Clara's task also fed Len's and Joanne's tasks, which were on the critical path:

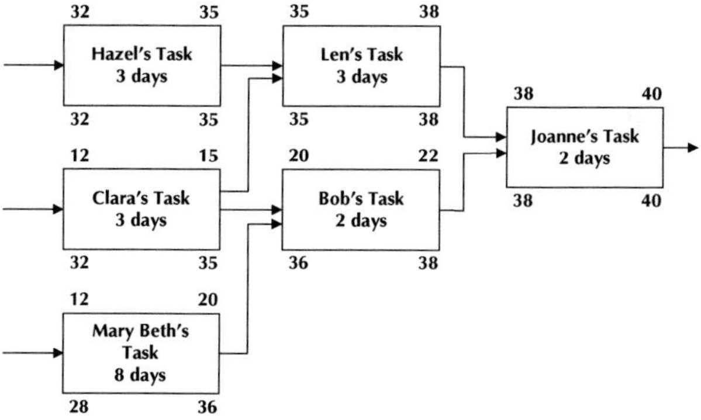

The amount of free float on Clara's task has not changed. It still has 5 days of free float. The free float determines how many days of free time exist between a task and its immediate successor. Based on the diagram here, Clara's task has 20 days of total float. There are 20 days of extra time along the path she is working before her work will influence the critical path. But she has only 5 days of free float. After 5 days, her delays will start creating delays for Bob.

The basic formula for free float is a simple one:

$$ESj - FSij - EFi = \text{Free float of i}$$

when ESj is the lowest of the successor start times

That caveat at the end is important. Clara has only 5 days of free float, not 20, despite the fact that one of her successor activities has an early start 20 days later. Bob's task is the earliest early start of her successor activities. His activity determines her free float.

Free float is important. As with total float, free float is an element of the project that the project manager can manage effectively. It is time that can be used to deploy resources more effectively, use them on other tasks, or reconsider the amount of effort involved. Time is a precious commodity on projects. By identifying free float, project managers have the opportunity to extract more time out of the network.

CHAPTER 3

THE ADVANCED RELATIONSHIPS

Not all relationships in the precedence diagram are finish-to-start. In some instances, it is not the completion of a task that drives the beginning of the next. Sometimes, the finish of one task triggers the finish of another. Sometimes the start of one task triggers the start of another. In rare instances, the start of one task may herald the impending finish of another. In most instances, project managers will work from the perspective that one task precedes another. In many situations, however, the project team and the project are better served by considering advanced relationships: start-start, finish-finish, and the somewhat esoteric start-finish.

Start-Start Relationships

Start-start relationships are predicated on the notion that the beginning of one task is driven by the beginning of another task. In a start-start relationship, the beginning of *i* drives the beginning of *j*. Often, some lag exists between the two. As with the finish-start relationship, start-start relationships can be driven by hard or soft logic. One of the main hindrances to using start-start relationships often is resource limitation. Finish-start relationships minimize resource conflicts by doing work serially. Start-start (and finish-finish) relationships often generate resource conflicts.

A hard logic example in a start-start relationship would be the relationship that exists between writing and editing. Writing must start, and then editing can begin. The two are inextricably linked. There is no way to begin the editorial process until writing has begun. In that example, it is evident that at least some small measure of lag must be put in place between the activities. That lag may be determined, in large part, by the writer. A prolific writer may be ready for editorial attention in a matter of days. A writer who moves more slowly may require a lot more lag before the editors are ready to begin their efforts.

Soft logic is common in start-start relationships. In an example of soft logic, two painters may have different responsibilities on a painting project. The trim painter may be responsible for "cutting in" the trim and the area around the trim. The wall painter is responsible for larger-scale painting. In this arrangement, the trim painter starts. One hour later, the wall painter begins. The hour of lag lets the trim painter get far enough ahead of the wall painter so that the two painters are not falling over each other. It also prevents them from dripping paint on one another.

In most academic presentations, the start-start relationship is displayed like this—

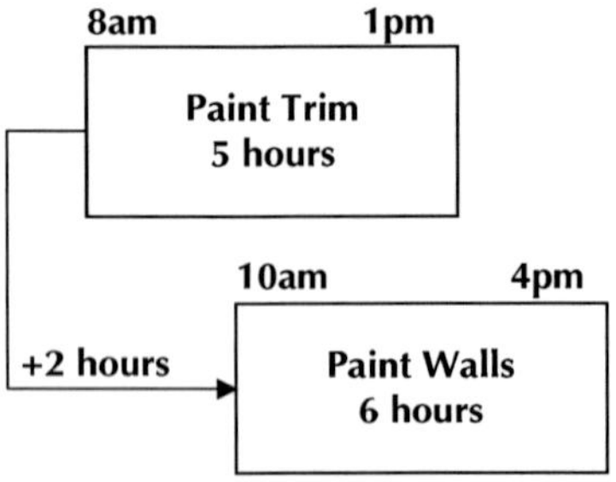

This clearly illustrates the relationship from the start of *i* to the start of *j*. If the start of the paint trim task is delayed, the start of the paint walls task will be delayed. The duration of the trim activity has nothing to do with the potential completion of the wall-painting task. The key is the start. If the paint trim task starts early, then the paint walls task also can get an earlier start. Although most textbooks present the information like this, most software packages do not. Those software packages that have adopted the time-scaled dependency diagram as a fundamental presentation style generate diagrams similar to the one above. In the precedence diagram view, however, (which often is misnamed the PERT view), software packages frequently display the relationship like this—

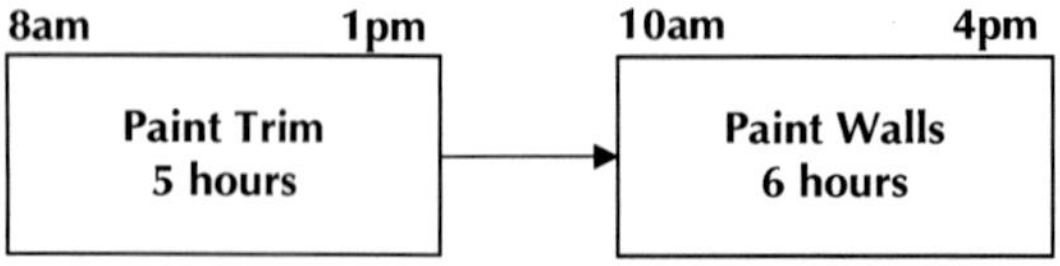

As a result, the relationships sometimes are misinterpreted. It is easy to see how the relationship could be misconstrued because there is no quick and easy way to see whether the relationship is finish-start, start-start, or finish-finish.

The key to a start-start relationship is to acknowledge that the start of the predecessor drives the start of the successor. Until *i* starts, *j* cannot start.

The only exception to that statement comes in a start-start relationship that uses lead time rather than lag time. Lead time drives the timing the other way, but does not change the fundamental relationship. In a situation with lead time, the statement would be couched as "X hours/days before *i* starts, *j* may start." *i* still drives the relationship. If *i* is late, then *j* will be late as well.

An example of a start-start relationship with lead time might involve the arrival of an important business executive from an overseas office. In this scenario, assume the executive prefers to determine some of the activities she will participate in at the last minute. The tasks might be "Mrs. Beasley visits the office" and "Prepare Mrs. Beasley's activities." The driving force in the network is going to be Mrs. Beasley's visit. The start of that task will drive the other tasks, even though the other tasks must happen first. For presentation, it would look something like this—

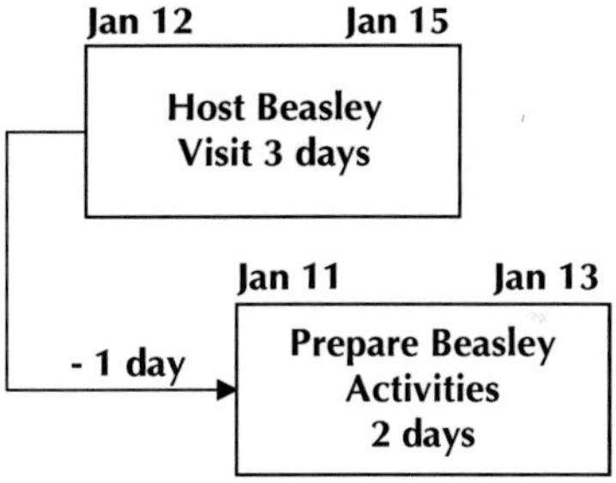

The reason this example works well here is that *if* Mrs. Beasley changes her schedule and her planned arrival time, the change will modify the schedule for preparing the activities. If she comes a day early, then the preparations must begin a day early. If she comes a week late, then the preparations may be postponed for a week. Although start-start relationships with lead time are not commonplace in most networks, they are appropriate in some situations.

Finish-Finish Relationships

For many tasks, the start time is not nearly as important as the finish time. One activity cannot finish until another finishes. A classic example is a holiday feast featuring a turkey. Everything—including guests and associated logistics—revolves around the preparation and completion of the turkey. To ensure that all the food makes it to the table hot and ready to go, it is crucial to time everything according to the stage at which the turkey has been cooked. But even in this simple example, lag becomes a crucial consideration. It is vital to ensure that the turkey has had time to cool before being placed on the table. Any cook will tell you that if you carve a turkey before it has cooled thoroughly, you wind up with "turkey dust" rather than turkey meat. The uncooled turkey cannot be carved properly without the lag time.

Properly done, the relationship for a holiday feast will look something like this—

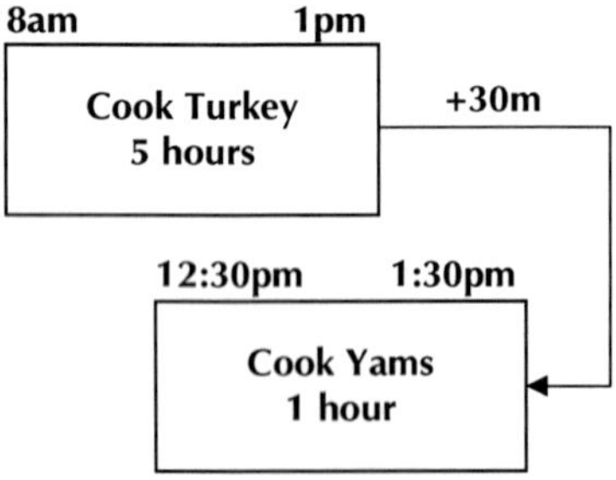

The relationship is being driven by the finish of the turkey. If the turkey is late, the yams will be late. It is a finish-to-finish relationship. The earlier example of writing and editing also could be applied here. Therefore, some analysts argue that there is little difference between a start-start and a finish-finish relationship. The difference, however, is dramatic. Using the turkey example, a start-start relationship would drive the start of the yams based on the start time of the turkey. As any cook knows, there are some signs to look for as a turkey roasts to identify whether it will be complete on time. Using the start-start relationship, those signs could not be taken into account when starting the yams. Their start time would be fixed the moment the cook turkey task began. With a finish-finish relationship, the scheduled finish time for the turkey drives the relationship and the schedule.

Other classic finish-finish relationships include—

- Software development must finish; then testing may finish.
- Laying down the linoleum must finish; then rolling the linoleum may finish.
- Sanding and washing the walls must finish; then painting the room may finish.
- Final requirements meetings with the customers must finish; then documenting the requirements may finish.

The finish-finish relationship often is used when customers expect many of their deliverables in a just-in-time format. If they want all their deliverables to be complete at a given point in time, it becomes vital to stage those deliverables based on the completion of a single, crucial deliverable.

As with the start-start relationship, the finish-finish relationship has instances in which lead time—not lag—is applied. The final scheduled delivery of a product or project often serves as a key moment in a project. The scheduled completion of a deliverable provides a mark against which the completion of other activities may be judged. Often, rental equipment secured for a specific project must be returned as quickly as possible. If the last work in product delivery involves packaging and other minor details, there is no reason to retain the rental equipment. The goal is to return the equipment to reduce overall project costs. The equipment may not be essential after the deliverable passes a certain point. In this case, the return rental equipment task may be a successor in a finish-finish relationship with the deliver final product task. After the final product delivery is scheduled for completion, a date can be established 1 week before completion to return the equipment. The relationship would look like this—

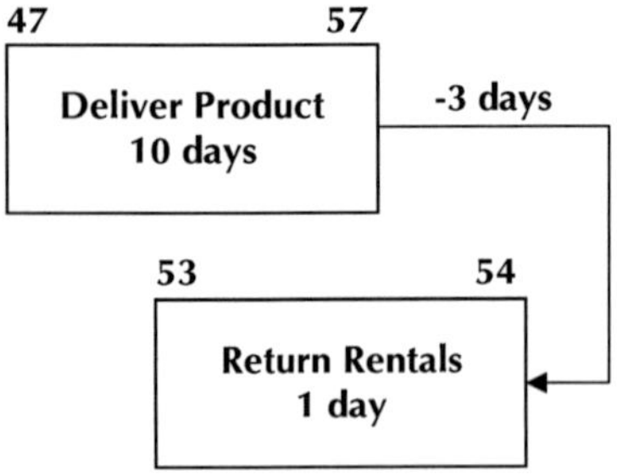

The scheduled completion of the product delivery task drives this relationship. If it is delayed, the completion of the rental return task must be delayed.

In many instances, recognizing that the end—not the beginning—of an activity is the key that can open the door to shorter schedules and more abbreviated turnaround times for projects. However, because finish-finish relationships drive parallel activities, they also generate greater risk by working teams toward the latest possible delivery times and by reducing recovery capability at the end of the task or project.

Start-Finish Relationships

In a start-finish relationship, one activity cannot finish until another activity is underway. The start time is not as important as the finish time in this type of relationship. The relationship between relay runners often is used to illustrate start-finish relationships. The first runner cannot finish until moments after the second runner has begun. It is the start of the second runner that will allow for the finish of the first.

This is considered a somewhat esoteric relationship in project management. In large part, that is because it is unusual, rare, and applied improperly more often than it is applied properly. Start-finish relationships are not available in certain software packages. Therefore, it is important to understand when they can be applied properly and when nothing else will work.

Specifically, start-finish relationships are most effective when they represent cause-and-effect relationships that are driven by the organization or that are common within a given set of processes and procedures. Start-finish relationships operate from the premise that *i* must start and then *j* may finish. The finish of the successor hinges on the beginning of its predecessor.

One classic business example of this relationship occurs when the project manager selection process is underway for a specified period of time before the proposal development process can be closed out. The company wants project managers to participate in the proposal process, even if a project manager has not been determined yet and even if the project manager will not have enough time to provide significant input to the process. Because management wants the project manager there, it assigns 2 weeks of lag to ensure that the project manager selection process has been underway for some time *before* the proposal phase finishes.

Ultimately, the relationship looks like this—

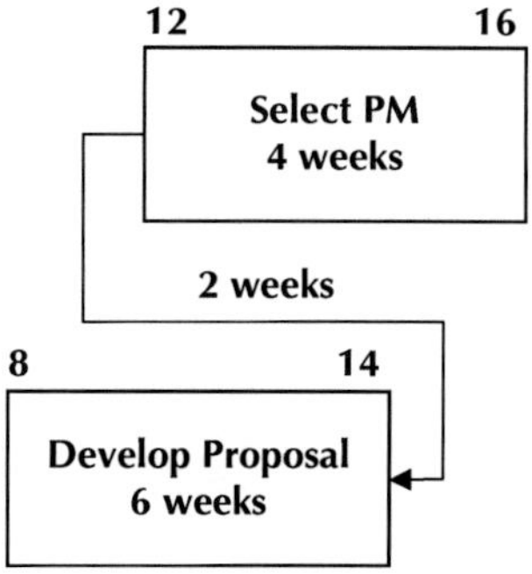

As soon as the relationship is established, questions ensue. "Isn't there another way to approach this? Couldn't we use a more conventional relationship?" The answer almost always is "yes." Through the effective use of lag and lead time, it is usually possible to approach the relationships in a way that affords greater clarity to team members. Still, there are those rare occasions where nothing else will do. In situations where the beginning of one activity drives the end of another, the start-finish relationship remains the best option.

The Hammock

In many organizations, task responsibility spans a group or organization. In those situations, the project manager does not need to see the details of the tasks being performed or the specific resource allocations for the work. Instead, assignment by work function or division is sufficient. The project manager need only know the task input and output and the duration of the work. That span of responsibility can be as simple as a series of three or four activities, or it can be an entire subproject.

The hammock is a common tool for separating these "spanned" activities from conventional work. What truly distinguishes the hammock from conventional work is the nature of the schedule itself. The hammock is more than a mere summary. It is an activity that hangs, like a hammock, between two specific points in time. Usually those points are the early start of one activity and the late finish of another.

The hammock affords project managers some scheduling advantages. If an organization has a division or department that is highly autonomous, the hammock grants the latitude required to ensure that the department or division functions with relative independence. In organizations in which the project manager has limited control, the hammock allows the project manager to identify the best-case start and the worst-case finish for a series of activities without appearing arbitrary about date selection.

Using the conventions discussed up to this point, the hammock has a start-start relationship with its predecessor. It also has a finish-finish relationship with its successor. It looks something like this—

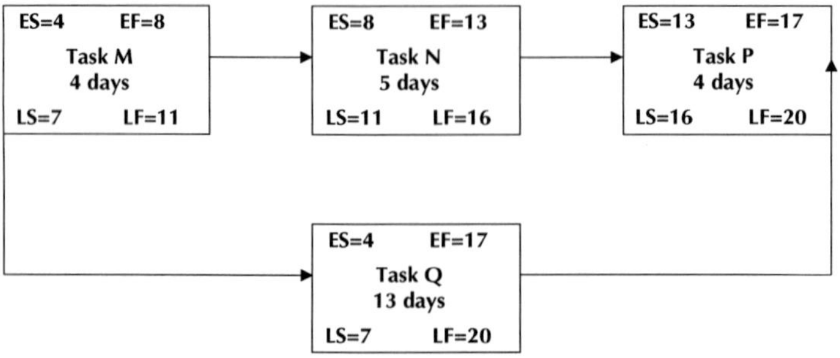

Task Q can start as early as its predecessor's early start. It can finish as late as its predecessor's late finish. Its duration will fluctuate with the start and end times of the predecessor and successor.

The hammock serves multiple functions. It can be used primarily for easy, effective summary schedule reporting. Organizations that need to see tasks M, N, and P as separate projects, or organizations that need to see tasks M, N, and P as subprojects may want to see the task groupings' total duration at any given point in time. The hammock provides quick and easy reporting. The hammock also may be used to capture management responsibility. If a manager wonders when his or her responsibilities begin and end, the hammock can serve as the management task for that group of activities.

Although more of the simpler project management software packages are allowing split activities, most of them will not build hammock activities effectively. High-end software such as Primavera Project Planner®, however, will track that information readily.

CHAPTER **4**

PRECEDENCE DIAGRAMMING AND THE TEAM

Precedence diagramming is a contact sport. It is not something that project managers should do in isolation or in a closed room with only one or two of their closest advisors. It serves the organization best when it supports the team and when the team is involved integrally with the implementation of the process and the practice. Too many precedence diagrams are generated in isolation. This results in a lack of team commitment to the schedules and a lack of understanding about approaches and procedures. Project managers must include team members in precedence diagram development to obtain their buy-in regarding the schedule.

Team Networking

Team networking is a challenge and can be an extraordinarily frustrating experience. Team efforts always generate different opinions about the best approach to doing the work. Numerous researchers recognize schedule conflict as the most intense conflict facing any project team.[9] Schedule conflict is a major source of differences of opinion with functional organizations, executive management, and customers. Much of the core conflict, however, derives from the project team's basic understanding of the schedule and its development.

In many organizations, project managers develop networks by gathering input from team members and by generating draft schedules for presentation at either the kickoff meeting or at a subsequent project gathering. Although that approach allows team members to provide input, it does not allow them to interact with others or to examine how those interactions will drive the rest of the project. It also means that the project manager loses a valuable opportunity for team building. Team-building activities that generate project deliverables provide a sense of value to both team members and to the project manager. Developing a schedule as a team requires expert facilitation and it requires key team players to be available.

Because schedules frequently are developed early in the project, some team members may not be available. In that case, the project manager must identify likely team members or representatives in requisite areas of expertise as the initial schedule is developed. It also is a good idea to ensure that the WBS or task list has been developed and reviewed before any group scheduling effort.

Preparing for Team Networking

Team networking is most effective when all the components have been put in place before the session. That means team members must have a prepared list of the tasks to be performed. They also need to provide a sense of when they will be available to do the session.

Logistically, team size will play a major role in the effectiveness of the precedence diagram exercise. For example, a team with 50 to 60 players will doom a precedence diagramming building effort. Keep the team size low by including representatives from each key center of expertise. Using team representatives keeps the team down to a manageable level and enables healthy discussion. Ideally, the team for a network diagramming session should have 10 or fewer members.

Room size and shape also create challenges. Because the diagram may span a significant area in a room, it is a good idea to allow ample space. A conservative space estimate is about 3 feet of available wall space for every 15 activities. A 300-activity network would require about 60 feet of wall space. A 75-activity network would consume about 15 feet of wall space. Cover as much wall space as necessary with flip chart (or "butcher") paper. This ultimately will become the "home" for the network diagram *in its draft form.*

The team must document the task list or work package level of the WBS task by task on Post-It® Notes. Team members will list one task per Post-It®. Team members can expedite the process by doing this before the meeting if they are working with a large task list. They also can document tasks at the meeting. Each task ultimately will be assigned to an "owner" who is responsible for placing the task at the appropriate point in the network diagram. Encourage team members to innovate. For example, a project manager may want to use different colors of Post-It® Notes for each functional area. Identifying functional areas by color makes it easier to identify utilization gaps and potential resource conflicts early in the process.

The following checklist provides guidance about whether a project manager is ready to lead a team networking session. Project managers who answer "yes" to each question know it is time for the team to start sorting through the diagram.

Team Networking Preparation Checklist	
Question	***Check here if the criterion has been met***
Has a comprehensive task list been developed?	
Have the team members reviewed the task list to ensure their work is fully represented?	
Has each task been documented on a separate Post-It® Note? (If desired, have the tasks for different organizations been documented on different colored Post-Its®?)	
Has a room been prepared with adequate space for wall documentation?	
Has the room been "wallpapered" with flip chart or "butcher" paper?	
Do you understand how to explain the process clearly?	

The last question in the checklist is critical. Explaining the process, in many cases, determines whether it succeeds or fails. The more clearly you explain how the process will be approached, the more effective the team will be. A simple explanation would be as follows—

We are about to lay down the process we will use for this project. Each team member has been given his or her tasks for the project on Post-It® Notes. You know the process better than anyone. You know what you need to get started, and you know what you are going to deliver when you finish a task. You also have the best perspective about how long the tasks are going to take (I realize that duration may change depending upon the input you get from others in this room).

I would like you to lay out your activities in the sequence in which they will be performed. Please modify the layout until the proper sequence is achieved as you receive input or provide input to others. Do not be afraid to put tasks in parallel sequence. Do not be concerned if it is not absolutely perfect. But try to ensure that you look for all the input you need to do your work as efficiently as possible.

What ensues is orchestrated mayhem. Team members will move their tasks onto the paper tentatively at first and with greater fervor as the effort progresses. They initially will seek compromise, but often, as the process becomes clear, significant differences of opinion will arise. It is far better to challenge the process on paper than to wait until the project is in full swing—even if the challenge causes tension within the team.

It is important for the facilitator to assure team members that it is normal to experience tension when building a network diagram. Team members who acknowledge that theirs is not the first team to encounter challenges and personal differences with this effort will be far more accepting of others' perspectives. And they must understand that although conflict is common, it does not give them license to abuse other team members. A difference in perspective is merely a difference in perspective. The critical issue with this process is to ensure that those differences are aired, clarified, and resolved before the project moves to implementation.

After the Post-It® Notes are arranged in a semblance of order, then, and only then, should team members draw the dependency lines. This is often the cathartic moment in the process. For many team members, this will become the point at which they realize they are committing themselves to deliverables, processes, and others within the organization. Both network logic and personal relationships evolve as the dependency lines are drawn.

The facilitator should encourage team members to think about the possibility of alternative relationships as they identify relationships between activities. Identify opportunities to generate start-start or finish-finish relationships with some lag if team members usually see their relationships as finish-start. In many instances, people can shave days (or even weeks) from the schedule by identifying alternative relationships.

Generating the lines between the relationships will provide ample insight into how the project will be performed. It also will help team members clarify how long their activities will take. Depending upon the deliverables and the input, duration times may change from task to task. This is a clarifying experience. The process gives team members the opportunity to finalize the task duration and to understand how that duration affects the project as a whole. It also will give you, the project manager, the last pieces of information required to load the schedule into a project management software package.

Before you release the team, ensure that it knows the implications of what it has done. Explain that you will generate the schedule in a more orderly format (such as a Gantt chart) after you have processed the information into the software package. Before you do that, however, ensure that the team is satisfied with the results and that team members agree about the layout and sequence of the work. The project manager also must carefully review each task to ensure its duration is finalized, its dependencies are clear, and the owner is identified clearly.

The entire process frequently will take 2 or 3 hours for a project with more than 150 tasks. It may take the greater part of a day for larger projects. In that time, team members gain unique insight about their roles in the project and how those roles connect with others. They understand where their deliverables fit in, and when they will be driving the schedule for the project as a whole. If the tasks are identified clearly by function (using the colored Post-It® Notes or some other means), team members also get a sense of the varying levels of responsibility associated with the different times in the project.

The project manager determines whether he or she will calculate the forward and backward pass with the team present. Some project managers will calculate the forward and backward pass with the team to create a sense of the overall schedule and to ensure that the schedule does not pass the customer's demand date. Others will release the team and generate the schedule using project management software.

After the project manager releases the team, the remaining level of effort is minimal. The WBS has been developed already and the information from it should be embedded into the software package already. All the project manager (or his or her scheduler) must do is to load the information from this session (durations, precedence relationships, lag, lead, and responsibility) into the software. After the information is loaded, a quick review of the schedule, duration, early and late starts, and resource loading should determine if the project schedule is feasible and reasonable.

Team Communication

Change inevitably will occur either at this early stage in the process or as the project moves forward. Changes are done through formal processes on most projects. But the network diagram is rarely updated. A classic example of this came in the analysis of a material management system implementation where the network diagram was posted across two walls of the project office. Halfway through a review of the diagram, someone asked the project manager, "Exactly where are we today?" The project manager laughed and replied, "That? We haven't updated that thing in 2 years."

The example illustrates the norm more than exception. Although Post-Its® may lose their "stick" over time, it is vital to retain the documentation. Updates are equally crucial. After the initial precedence diagram is built, there rarely is cause to build it anew or do a total overhaul. Although most software packages generate network diagrams across dozens of sheets of paper that must be trimmed, sliced, and taped together, an update rarely spans more than a handful of activities, at least in the near term. Therefore, project managers should update the network diagram on-line with computer tools, and print the changed pages. Project managers also can use a screen capture to retool the image as a bitmap, and send it out on-line. Either way, team members do not need to see the entire network and do not need to "rewallpaper" the room.

With the advent of time-scaled precedence diagrams in many of the tools, people are tempted to use what some call a "modified Gantt view" to present the precedence information. The example below illustrates the key challenge associated with that approach:

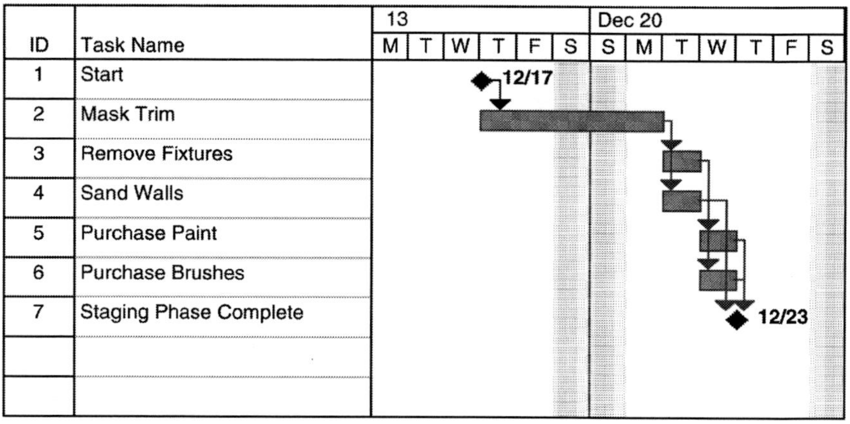

In this example, the sand walls task is the predecessor of the purchase brushes task, and the remove fixtures task is the predecessor of the purchase paint task. It is difficult, however, to tell which concurrent activities are related to which other activities. The format becomes even more challenging when there are 50, 100, or 200 tasks. The use of this perspective is extremely limited.

Summary

What works best? That is largely a function of the individuals and the organization. Different groups and different people have broadly different perspectives about what will and what will not work. Precedence diagramming affords a clear, easy-to-understand means to illustrate relationships and to determine the total project duration. It also opens the door to team building and mutual understanding of the schedule.

The fundamental process involves five steps:

- Build the task list or work breakdown structure.
- Assign task responsibility during or before the meeting.

- Network the tasks and consider different colored Post-Its® for different functional organizations.
- Draw the relationships before releasing the team.
- Document the conclusions in the project management software or elsewhere.

By developing the network as a team and by working together to establish individual and shared project responsibility for the project, the project process will be clearer to the team and the project approach will become a shared undertaking.

People usually do not argue with their own data. The more the project manager can do to create the network, the schedule, and the process as a joint effort, the higher the probability of project success.

ENDNOTES

[1] Project Management Institute Standards Committee. *A Guide to the Project Management Body of Knowledge.* Upper Darby, Penn.: Project Management Institute, 2000, p. 204.

[2] Stuckenbruck, Linn. *The Implementation of Project Management: The Professional's Handbook.* Reading, Mass.: Addison-Wesley, 1981, p. 121.

[3] Dreger, J. Brian. *Project Management: Effective Scheduling.* New York: Van Nostrand Reinhold, 1992, p. 35.

[4] Cleland, David and William King. *Project Management Handbook.* New York: Van Nostrand Reinhold, 1988, p. 358.

[5] Goldratt, Eliyahu. *The Critical Chain.* Great Barrington, Mass.: North River Press, 1997.

[6] *The Four-Hour House,* San Diego Building Industry Association, 1991.

[7] Dreger, J. Brian. *Project Management: Effective Scheduling.* New York: Van Nostrand Reinhold, 1992.

[8] Project Management Institute Standards Committee. *A Guide to the Project Management Body of Knowledge.* Upper Darby, Penn.: Project Management Institute, 2000, p. 202.

[9] Thamhain, Hans and David Wilemon. "Conflict in Project Life Cycles." *Sloan Management Review* Summer (1975): 31-50.

GLOSSARY

activity-on-arc
See precedence diagramming method.

activity-on-arrow (AOA)
See arrow diagramming method.

arrow diagramming method (ADM)
ADM is a network diagramming technique in which activities are represented by arrows. The tail of the arrow represents the start of the activity; the head of the arrow represents the finish of the activity. The length of the arrow does not represent the expected duration of the activity. Activities are connected at points called nodes (usually drawn as circles) to illustrate the sequence in which the activities are expected to be performed. *It also is called* activity-on-arrow.

backward pass
The backward pass is a calculation of late finish and late start dates for uncompleted portions of all network activities. It is determined by working backward through the network logic from the project's end date. *Also see* forward pass.

Where i is the predecessor and j is the successor, $LFi =$

$LFj - DURj - FSij$

$LFj - FFij$

$LFj - DURj - SSij + DURi$

$LFj - SFij + DURi$

discretionary dependency
This is a dependency defined by preference, rather than necessity. *It also is called* preferred logic, preferential logic, *or* soft logic.

early finish date (EF)

The EF is the earliest possible point in time when the uncompleted portions of an activity (or the project) can end based on network logic and any schedule constraints. It may change as the project progresses or as changes are made to the project plan. It is used in the critical path method.

early start date (ES)

The ES is the earliest possible point in time when the uncompleted portions of an activity (or the project) can begin, based on network logic and any schedule constraints. It may change as the project progresses or as changes are made to the project plan. It is used in the critical path method.

finish-to-finish (FF)

FF is the relationship in a precedence diagramming method network in which one activity must end before the successor activity can end. *Also see* logical relationship.

finish-to-start (FS)

FS is the relationship in a precedence diagramming method network in which one activity must end before the successor activity can start. It is the most commonly used relationship in the precedence diagramming method. *Also see* logical relationship.

float

Float also is called *slack, total float,* and *total slack.* It is the late start minus the early start of an activity in network diagrams. It also is the late finish minus the early finish.

forward pass

The forward pass is the calculation of the early start and early finish dates for the uncompleted portions of all network activities. *Also see* network analysis and backward pass.

Where i is the predecessor and j is the successor, $ESj =$

$ESi + DURi + FSij$

$ESi + DURi + FFij - DURj$

$ESi + SSij$

$ESi + SFij - DURj$

free float

Free float is the amount of time that an activity may be delayed without delaying the early start of any immediately succeeding activities. *Free float also is called* secondary float.

free slack
See free float.

Gantt chart
A Gantt chart is a graphic display of schedule-related information. Generally, activities or other project elements are listed down the left side of the chart, dates are shown across the top, and activity durations are displayed against the x and y axes as date-placed horizontal bars. This chart is named after its developer, Henry Gantt.

hammock
A hammock is a group of related activities that is shown as one aggregate activity and reported at a summary level. It may or may not have an internal sequence.

hard logic
See mandatory dependency.

lag
Lag is the modification of a logical relationship in a schedule so that there is a delay in the successor task. For example, in a finish-to-start dependency with a 5-day lag, the successor activity cannot start until 5 days after the predecessor has finished. *Also see* lead.

late finish date (LF)
LF is the latest possible point in time that an activity may end without a delay in the project finish date. LF is used in the critical path method. *Also see* late start date.

late start date (LS)
LS is the latest possible point in time that an activity may begin without delaying the project finish date. It is used in the critical path method. *Also see* late finish date.

lead
Lead is the modification of a logical relationship in a schedule so that there is an acceleration of the successor task. For example, in a

finish-to-start dependency with a 5-day lead, the successor activity can start 5 days before the predecessor has finished. *Also see* lag.

logic diagram
See network diagram.

mandatory dependency
This is a dependency inherent in the nature of the work being done, such as a physical limitation. *It also is called* hard logic.

network diagram
This is a schematic display of the logical relationships of project activities, usually drawn from left to right to reflect project chronology. *It also is called* logic diagram and often is incorrectly referred to as a PERT chart.

precedence diagramming method (PDM)
This is a network diagramming technique in which activities are represented by boxes (or nodes) and are linked by precedence relationship lines to show the sequence in which the activities are to be performed. The nodes are connected with arrows to show the dependencies. Four types of relationships are possible: finish-to-finish, finish-to-start, start-to-finish, and start-to-start. *It also is called* activity-on-arc.

preferential logic
See discretionary dependency.

program evaluation and review technique (PERT)
PERT is an event-oriented, probability-based network analysis technique used to estimate project duration when there is a high degree of uncertainty with the individual activity duration estimates. PERT applies the critical path method to a weighted average duration estimate. The formula is as follows:

$$\frac{O+(4ML)+P}{6}$$

where O = optimistic time, ML = most likely time, and P = pessimistic time.

slack

See float.

soft logic

See discretionary dependency.

start-to-finish

This is a relationship in a precedence diagramming method network in which one activity must start before the successor activity can finish.

start-to-start

This is a relationship in a precedence diagramming method network in which one activity must start before the successor activity can start.

total float

See float.

total slack

See float.

work breakdown structure (WBS)

The WBS is a deliverable-oriented grouping of project elements that organizes and defines the total scope of the project. Each descending level is an increasingly detailed definition of a project component. Project components may be products or services.